PHOBIAS

I0409581

Gone In 1 Hour

By

Regan Forston Ct.Ht.

Disclaimer

All the material contained in this book is provided for educational purposes only. No responsibility can be taken for any results or outcomes resulting from the use of this material. While every attempt has been made to provide information that is both accurate and effective, the author does not assume any responsibility for the accuracy or use/misuse of this information. The techniques taught in this book while miraculous at times are not a panacea. Anyone with severe emotional issues should seek a health care professional.

Acknowledgements

I really want to thank my dear friend Davar who let me spend several months at his beach house in Baja, Mexico to write this book. I also want to thank all my wonderful clients who have allowed me to help them heal from some of their life's challenges. Helping you heal has in turn helped me to heal my life's issues.

I want to thank Miss Kerri Zeineddini for her inspiration and support in motivating me to write this book.

Table Of Contents

PREFACE

What wonderful times we are in. With all the advances in our knowledge on how our bodies and minds work, new therapies are constantly being developed. New advances in "Energy Medicine" are changing the way we heal emotional trauma. Dr. Oz on his recent TV show said that energy medicine is the future of medicine.

One of the first breakthroughs has been in how we cure people of phobias. It is so simple a 5 year old can learn the procedure. The process you are going to learn about is fast becoming the most used modality in the world for treatment of fears, phobias, PTST {Post Traumatic Stress) and any other stress related issues that people have. It is called EFT which stands for "Emotional Freedom Technique." It is also called "Tapping." You may have heard it discussed on your favorite talk show recently as it has been all over the news. Dr. Oz has been using the technique for the last 10 years for his clients. He says he uses EFT because "it works." He even has a tutorial on his website to teach people how to do EFT.

This new therapeutic process has just been accepted as a viable form of therapy by the American Psychological Association because of all the positive studies showing not only visible proof, but physiological proof, as well.

You are about to learn a healing modality that is safe, non evasive, and has miraculous results. In the last chapter of this book, you will do your own personal therapy session and rid yourself of your phobia.

Who This Book is For

The book was written for people who have phobias, but **don't** have access to a mental health professional, or **don't** have sufficient funds to afford therapy.

If money is not an issue, and you have easy access to an EFT professional in your area, I would suggest having them take away your phobia, only because it is one step better than doing it all by yourself.

If money isn't as an issue and you don't have access to a professional in your area, then I want you to email me. I will get in touch with you to set an appointment for a phone or Skype session. Phone or Skype sessions work quite well for curing phobias.

I say, why pay me when you can easily learn to do this yourself. One way or the other, whether you do it yourself, or I do it for you, that pesky phobia is going to be gone.

Why Write This Book

After five years of helping my clients get rid of their phobias, it came to me that it was the client themselves that did the curing. Whether I am helping them with a Skype or phone session or am sitting right next to them, all I am is a guide telling them what to do. My clients would tap where I said to tap and repeat what I told them to say, and like magic, their phobias would disappear.

I thought, if I write down the simple procedure in book form, I can reach thousands of people who can in the privacy of their own space, cure themselves of their phobias.

The other reason I wrote this book is to help you in other areas of your life. Once you know the tapping procedure it can be used in all areas of your life where you have excess emotion left over from experienced trauma and stress.

Chapter 1: Overview of this Book

"Fear is a tyrant and a despot, more terrible than the rack, more potent than the snake."

---- Edgar Wallace - The Clue of the Twisted Candle (1916)

Here is how this is going to work. You read this book, educating yourself and getting an idea on how and why you have a fear or phobia. You will realize that you are not unique because millions of people have them. Once I give you an understanding of phobias I will teach you the simple technique used to get rid of them. Then you will do your own personal therapy session to get rid of your phobia. I will take you step by step through the process.

If you just don't have the confidence or just don't want to do this by yourself, I will be able to help you by doing a personal session for you.

Learning EFT is not brain science, I have taught it to children. When you learn this, I encourage you to teach it to your children and your friends.

Sharing Tapping with Others

I taught EFT to an actress friend of mine in Hollywood. I was on a movie set at the *El Capitan* movie theatre across from *Grauman's Chinese Theatre* on Hollywood Blvd. I was working for a few days on *The Muppet 2011 Movie*. I noticed an actress who kept rubbing her temples and every minute or so groaned in pain. I approached her and said I see you are in some pain. She replied, "Major pain." I told her I was a therapist and had a quick and easy technique to take away pain and asked if I could help. She said you can try, but I get these migraines all the time and nothing works.

I sat her down in one of the movie seats at the theatre, had her close her eyes and look at an" imaginary pain meter" in her mind's eye. The scale went from 1-10. I asked her if she could visualize the meter in her mind. She said yes. Then I asked her how high on that scale her pain was. She said it was very high, an 8 or 9.

Since she didn't know how to tap, I did it for her. I did three rounds of the tapping while having her repeat these words at each of the points I tapped on, *"Even though, I have this horrible headache and it is at an 8 or 9, I completely and deeply accept, and love myself."*

After the first round, she again checked her inner meter and her pain was at a 7, after the second round it was at a 4. When we finished the third round, I asked her to tell me how the pain was. She had her eyes closed, and I could see her searching for the pain. She kept on searching as if she knew it had to be there somewhere, but she couldn't find it.

The look on her face was one of peace and bewilderment. We smiled at each other. She gave me a warm thankful hug, and I was on my way. Later in the day, after lunch she found me and said, "I can't believe it. My headache vanished and hasn't come back." She wanted to know more about how I made her pain go away, so, between scenes, I taught her how to tap.

About a year later I was on the movie set *J. Edgar*, a Clint Eastwood movie, playing the lawyer of a woman on trial for subversion. She saw me at dinner and asked me if I remembered her. I pretended I did because at first she did look somewhat familiar. I had been on so many movie sets, and you meet so many people, mostly for a day and then usually never see them again.

As soon as she started recounting the headache story, I remembered her. She said that she got so excited about learning more about tapping that she found a teacher of EFT to help her learn more about it. She said not only does she have a way to relieve her pain, but now helps her friends, family, and even people on movie sets get rid of their headaches. She is doing just what I did for her, sharing new knowledge with others.

I am hoping that some of you who read this book will go out and do the same. It is time to share the wealth.

Chapter 2: Phobias Can Be Life Threatening

"Men fear death as children fear to go in the dark."

---- Francis Bacon

What if you had a fear of water and you saw your child drowning? What if your 2 year old had climbed out the bedroom window onto the roof three floors up and you had a phobia of heights? Can you see how having a phobia can lead to tragedy? Here is a story that happened to a client of mine.

Case History

Lydia the Doctors Wife

Issue: Fear of Driving Freeways

Lydia was the wife of a retired doctor. She was a referral from another client. I met her in her home, a very nice home in Costa Mesa California. As I walked into her home, I felt love. I don't how describe how I felt love in the air, but I did. The way she looked, the way she carried herself, the calm and friendly way she spoke, I could tell this was a wonderful human being.

She asked me to come upstairs to meet her husband. As I got to the top of the stairs, I could see her husband directly to my right. He was in a hospital bed and had a number of tubes and devices hooked up to him, but he didn't look too sick. He smiled and shook my hand. We spoke only briefly and then his daughter came in, a beautiful woman that looked to be in her 40's. She was there to take over the care of her father so Lydia and I could start therapy.

Lydia was an eloquent looking woman from Nicaragua. She landed a job as a housekeeper for this doctor. When the doctor's wife died about 15 years later, the doctor ended up following in love with her, and they got married. They had now been married for 8 years. She told me that he was the most kind and thoughtful man she had ever known.

Here's what happened to her husband. A few years ago he got a stomach disease and had to have his stomach operated on. He is a doctor himself, so he made sure he was in a good hospital with a well qualified surgical team. Even so it couldn't prevent an awful thing happening to him. The surgeon removed the wrong half of his stomach. Now he didn't have a stomach and had to be fed through a tube for the rest of his life. Lydia took him home so she could give him the best care. She had been by his side caring for him now for over two years. He had lasted much longer than they said he would last. What a wonderful woman to sacrifice so much of her own needs to care for her dying husband.

One day they couldn't find his important pills. He had to have these pills to prevent him from having a seizure. She called his doctor and had him prescribe some more of his medication. That was fine. Their pharmacy was only 10 minutes away. This is where her phobia kicked in. She had a horrible fear of driving on freeways or on any streets that were very steep. Her daughter had always gone to the pharmacy for her but she couldn't reach her. Now what was she going to do. He needed his pills fast.

She jumped in her car and figured somehow she would face her fear and drive the freeway. She was ok until she started going down the freeway on-ramp. At that point she felt a full blown panic attack coming on. She was driving slow and swerving as she tried to control her panic. Her heart felt it would jump out of her chest. Other drivers were honking and yelling at her, making it even worse. She finally was able to pull off the road. She started crying and now her mind raced with what might happen is she didn't return in time.

She composed herself and called her daughter again. Her daughter said she was an hour away, so her daughter called a friend of hers who lived close by. Her friend rushed over, picked up Lydia, and saved the day.

They raced home with the prescription, and her husband was just fine, thank God.

After this incident, she knew she had to do something about her phobia. If she didn't, it could cost her husband his life. One of her friends was a client of mine, and when she called to tell her friend about her dilemma, her friend referred her to me.

Now here I am with Lydia, and I can see her visibly shaken from just recounting her story. When Lydia finished telling me this very emotional story, I assured her that we could take care of her problem and not to worry.

I had her get comfortable, and I took about 45 minutes to teach her how to do the tapping. Then I had her close her eyes and relive the freeway on-ramp incident in her mind one more time. As she relived it, her emotional level went right to a 10. She was so emotional she couldn't tap on the points herself, so I did the tapping for her. After three rounds of tapping, we got her emotional level to a 7. At least now when I had her relive the incident she didn't start crying and shaking. I made an appointment for two days later for us get in her car and retrace her way to the freeway.

When I returned two days later she was ready to give it a try, so we got in her car, and off we went. She said the first session had helped somewhat; she could feel that she wasn't as afraid as she was before. That gave her courage to get in the car with me.

She drove just fine until we got near the freeway on-ramp and then her body started to shake. I have to say I got a little panicky myself, she was really shaking. I had her pull over immediately. We sat there and taped for about 20 minutes, and we got her emotional needle down to a 3. She said it was strange how she felt. She could feel her fear evaporating. This time we gave it another try. It was a bit shaky for about a mile and then it evened out. We got all the way to the pharmacy. I spent another hour with her, driving back and forth to the pharmacy 3 times.

When we returned she was so happy and thankful she cried, and I got one of the most genuine hugs I had ever had. In the following months, she was able to drive to the pharmacy all by herself.

I got an email from her a few weeks ago telling me her husband finally lost his fight. I went to see her a few days ago. She is managing, but you can tell her loss is great. I will help her with some grief therapy when things settle down in a few months.

Lydia's success in overcoming her phobia is typical of my clients. I am hoping we can do the same for you.

Chapter 3: Phobias

"The oldest and strongest emotion of mankind is fear."

--- H.P. Lovecraft

Fears and Phobias, we all have at least one; some of us have a whole bunch of them. They cause us anything from slight agitations to major problems. They can totally run and ruin our lives. Until now, the only way to get rid of these monsters was to go through long and expensive therapy. Not having the money or the time to do anything about them, we suffer through them the best we can.

Is a Fear the Same as a Phobia?

For the purposes of this book, when I use the words fears or phobias, I am talking about the same thing. Technically, there is a difference between a "fear" and a "phobia," but only a trained therapist would need to know the difference. In Hypnotherapy College, we made a distinction between the two for therapeutic reasons.

We were taught, if you were afraid of something and knew what the cause of your fear was, then we call that a "fear." If you haven't a clue why you have your fear, then we call it a phobia.

For EFT to be effective, it is not essential that a person knows what caused the phobia.

For the purposes of this book, let's just say fears and phobias are basically the same thing. I can then use the words interchangeably and not confuse you.

Fears and phobias come in all shapes and sizes. Some of them can be very traumatic, and others seem very silly to us. The traumatic ones can cause our lives to be miserable. The silly phobias may be just an annoyance, but wouldn't you agree that life would be better without them? Until recently, the world view was that we are stuck with our fears and phobias, and just have to make the best of it. The good news is we are in a new era; the 21st Century and things are changing. The new discoveries on how the body's energy works is changing the whole paradigm of healing.

The biggest discoveries have been in Energy Medicine and Energy Psychology. These two emerging fields are growing by leaps and bounds. We are learning how to manipulate and fix disrupted energies in the body, causing rapid and sometimes instant healing for a myriad of health issues.

We now believe that fears and phobias are "stuck energy." This stuck energy can be unstuck rather easily, and when it gets unstuck your fear or phobia simply vanishes as if it were never even there. In a few minutes, you are going to learn how to rid yourself of that nasty, pesky fear or phobia by just using the tips of your fingers. I know this sounds strange, but it is not. It works very fast in most cases.

Defining Phobias

These next few pages were written by a Kendra Perry for "About.com." The following article she wrote will help you understand what phobias are.

Definitions Phobias Defined

According to the American Psychiatric Association, a phobia is an irrational and excessive fear of an object or situation. In most cases, the phobia involves a sense of endangerment or a fear of harm. For example, those suffering from agoraphobia fear being trapped in an inescapable place or situation.

Symptoms of Phobias

Phobic symptoms can occur through exposure to the fear object or situation, or sometimes simply thinking about the feared object can lead to a response. Common symptoms associated with phobias include:

- Dizziness

- Breathlessness

- Nausea

- A sense of unreality

Types of Phobias

There are three types of phobias:

1. Social phobias—fear of social situations.

2. Agoraphobia—fear of being trapped in an inescapable place or situation

3. Specific phobias—fear of a specific object (such as snakes).

There are four major types of specific phobias:

1.   The natural environment—fear of lightning, water, storms, etc.

2.   Animal—fear of snakes, rodents, spiders, etc.

3.   Medical—fear of seeing blood, receiving injections, visiting a doctor, etc.

4.   Situational—fear of bridges, leaving the home, driving, etc.

Prevalence of Phobias

Phobias are actually quite common, affecting more than 10% of the U.S. population. Phobias are the most common mental disorder in the United States, but far more women than men are affected by phobias. In many cases, people are able to recognize that their fear is irrational and, therefore, take steps to overcome their phobia. According to the Diagnostic and Statistical

Manual of Mental Disorders, only about 10 percent of reported cases become lifelong phobias.

Treatments for Phobias

There are a number of treatment approaches for phobias. The effectiveness of a treatment depends on the individual and the type of phobia. These are just a few potential phobia treatments:

In **exposure treatments**, the patient is exposed to the fear object in order to help them overcome their fear. One type of **exposure treatment** is flooding, in which the patient is confronted by the fear object for an extended length of time without the opportunity to escape. The goal of this method is to help the individual face their fear and realize that the fear object will not harm them.

Another method often used in phobia treatment is **counter-conditioning**. In this method, the patient is taught a new response to the fear object. Rather that panic in the face of the feared object or situation, the client learns relaxation techniques to replace anxiety and fear. This new behavior is incompatible with the previous panicked response, so the phobic response gradually fades. **Counter-conditioning** is often used with patients who are unable to handle exposure treatments.

$$***$$

In the above article, the modalities she mentions are helpful and still used in helping people overcome their phobias, but with the new findings in "Energy Medicine," newer and quicker ways of therapy are emerging. Wouldn't you like to get over your phobia in a few hours as compared to a few months or years? Sure you would, not to mention all the money you would save on therapy costs.

At the end of 2012, EFT was formally accepted by the American Psychological Association. Since it has been given validity, thousands of new practitioners are beginning to use it to cure people of their phobias.

Case History

Doctor Stevens

Issue: Fear of Answering the Phone

Again, if you are not the one with this fear, you may think it is silly, but this fear was causing my client some serious problems. When I tell you his story, you will understand how he came to have this fear.

I knew this man from a friend of mine. I was at a party of his a few years ago. Dr. Stevens was a very successful doctor and lived in a 7,000 square foot home on the top of a hill overlooking Hollywood California. He had a 70,000 Mercedes, a beautiful wife; two vacation homes and two pure bred Saint Bernard dogs. He had a life that I envied. I got to know him. He was a most personable fellow.

When he found out I was a Hypnotist, he had a million and one questions. It is very common in my profession for people to ask me lots of questions about how Hypnosis works. I left the party that night, and as I was leaving he asked me for my business card. That was the last I saw of him for two years.

About two years later, I get a call from him asking me to see him for therapy. I said I would be happy to drive the 90 miles to Hollywood to see him. I do that for all my clients; I make house calls. Anyway, he said he wasn't in Hollywood anymore; he was living in an apartment in downtown LA.

When I met him the next day, he gave me a warm handshake, got me a glass of water, and began telling me his story.

Remember what I told you a minute ago in this story, how he was living on top of the world? Well now he told me he had lost his home, as a matter of fact, this apartment where he was belonged to a friend who was letting him stay there for a few weeks.

He no longer had his medical practice. He had closed both of his clinics. His Mercedes was gone; he didn't even have a car at all now. He had to give up his two dogs; his wife was in Federal Prison, and he only had $30 to his name.

As you can imagine, my jaw dropped. He could see I was shocked, and then began to tell me his story. It seems that he was accused of being a drug dealer, of using his doctor's license to sell drugs on the internet. It was national news, but I had never seen it.

He was charged with over twenty counts of selling drugs and was looking at a lot of years in prison.

As it turned out, during the trial, his wife came clean and admitted it was she who was the guilty party. She had conspired with another man to use her husband's medical license to illegally sell drugs on the internet. Dr.

Stevens didn't have a clue what was going on. He didn't even know she was a prescription drug addict. She was also using his license to prescribe drugs for herself. He had to use all his resources to defend himself, over a million dollars in legal fees.

He lost his practice because he couldn't defend himself and continue practicing at the same time, besides, this was a high profile trial and as he said it, "who wants to go see a doctor who is in a court defending himself on drug charges."

His fear of answering the phone stemmed from having to face his family, friends, and business associates. When they would call he was constantly assuring them that he was not guilty. He got so tired of trying to convince them of his innocence. He knew he was innocent, but you know how being accused of a crime, is the same as being guilty in the eyes of a lot of us.

Many innocent people's lives have been ruined by false accusations. In this case justice was served as he was found not guilty of any wrong doing.

He was not guilty, but look at all he lost proving his innocence. Who wouldn't need some therapy after going through what he did.

When Dr. Stevens's phone would ring now, his anxiety level would go through the roof, and he just couldn't get himself to answer it. His stress meter was at a 9. All I had to do with him was 4 rounds of tapping, and having him say, *"even though, I have this horrible fear of answering the phone because of the humiliation I feel, I completely and deeply accept and love myself."* That was all it took. He went to a zero, and it has never come back.

I worked with him further for his other issues using both Hypnosis and EFT. It is now two years later, and I am happy to say that he is doing superb. He has a nice place near the beach, a new BMW, he had a health product he helped develop get approved by the FDA and has two new clinics going. In a few years, he will be a millionaire again. Oh, he also has several beautiful women pursuing him.

Chapter 4: How We Develop Phobias

*"All of us are born with a set of instinctive fears--
of falling, of the dark, of lobsters, of falling on lobsters in
the dark, or speaking before a Rotary Club, and of the
words "Some Assembly Required."*
---- Dave Barry

I have found that most phobias come from:

- An experienced traumatic event

- An imagined traumatic event

- A past life memory of a traumatic event

- Things we hear and see

- Who knows where it came from

- Experienced Traumatic Event

Let's say you have a fear of snakes because when you were 7 and taking a bath, your older brother threw a snake in the tub with you. You screamed, and in your haste to get out of the tub, hit your head on the towel rack, and cut your head open. If you have ever had a head wound, you know blood is everywhere. Usually, it is not as bad as it looks, but when you run out of the bathroom naked with blood all over your face screaming "Snake, snake," and your mom sees you; before you know it, you are on your way to the hospital in an ambulance.

Having never been in a hospital before, you are further traumatized hearing your mom screaming at the nurses that if they don't do something quick you are going to die. Then realizing that you missed your last confession at church on Sunday, and if you die you think you are going to hell; that is a lot for a 7 year old to handle. Not to mention the callous nurse who jams a needle in your head, to numb it, so it doesn't hurt when they stitch you up. It's no wonder you have a fear of snakes. You may also now have a fear of hospitals, nurses, needles, and death.

I had a phobia of dogs that lasted until I was 40 years old. It was caused from having two vicious dogs on my paper route when I was 9 years old. This was before leash laws. I remember the paperboy from the rival newspaper showing me the bite on his leg he had just got from the dog at my customer's house: the same house I was about to deliver a newspaper to.

I tried to be as quiet as I could, but the dog saw me. I ran as fast as I could, escaping with only teeth marks in my jeans. That was all it took for me to be afraid of dogs for 31 more years.

Imagined Traumatic Event

Isn't it fascinating how powerful our minds are? It is possible to feel like you experienced an awful event even though it was only created in your imagination. This is especially true of young children. Young children's minds accept what they see and hear as real. They have not learned discrimination yet to tell fantasy from reality.

I remember when some older boys told me "little people" lived in this tiny cave near the railroad tracks. They told me that these little people would come out at dusk and find little kids to eat. I was scared for years to go near that cave. I would go the long way around through the woods to avoid being eaten by them. I had dreams of these scary "little people" chasing me. I was even afraid of a dwarf clown that I saw at a circus my father took me to.

Some things embedded in our subconscious at a young age stay there as truth. Even when we get to the age of learning discrimination, it can be hard to shake what we used to think of as truth. I have seen grown adults acting like little kids when exposed to their phobias.

Phobias from Things We Hear and See

We develop fears from things we hear. All of us have heard that 13 is an unlucky number. That doesn't bother most of us, but to a very suggestible person, 13 becomes a number they stay away from like a plague. I heard of a woman who passed up a high paying job because her office would have been on the 13th floor of a big downtown building.

We don't have to have something physically happen to us to develop a phobia. For instance, if you saw a movie when you were young about a shark that always attacked and killed kids who swam in the ocean. A certain percentage of children will develop a fear of sharks or a fear of swimming or both.

Phobias with No Known Cause

There are many people that have phobias and have no idea where their fear originated from. Sometimes it is suppressed memory. I can use Hypnosis to regress them back in their minds to an earlier time in their lives, and sometimes they will uncover a suppressed memory of a traumatic event. If we find the event that caused their fear, sometimes just figuring out where it came from will cause the phobia to go away.

Remember, with EFT it is not crucial to find the cause. You can "tap" it away still with a little extra work. Don't get overly caught up in having to find the root of your phobia.

When we don't know where the phobia originated, and we do the taping, and the phobia won't go away, we try one last thing. Luckily, for a good number of people, we find the solution there. Read on.

Phobias from Past Lives

I know for some of you, what I am about to say is going to sound a bit strange, and unbelievable, but I have to include this in the book. Why? Because in my experience, and many other Hypnotherapists; we've discovered that some of our clients phobias seem to have come from something they experienced in a previous lifetime.

Dr. Weiss one of the best known Psychiatrists and Hypnotherapists in the world has been studying this phenomenon for over 20 years. His book, "*Many Lives Many Masters*" tells the story of his adventure in the discovery of past life traumas.

As I understand it, it all began when a client, an older gentleman came to him with the complaint of a constant pain in his leg. He had this pain ever since he could remember. He always walked with a limp. He had been seen by doctors many times, taken pain medications, tried physical therapy, none of which were successful in relieving the constant pain in his leg. Finally, his doctor had a thought, maybe the pain was psychosomatic. Was it possible that some accident or trauma he experienced from early childhood was causing his mind to feel pain in his leg? Maybe it was all in his head the doctor thought.

I do know the mind can create pain where there is none. A colleague had a client who didn't believe in hypnosis. The client challenged my colleague to prove that hypnosis was real.

My colleague took the challenge. As it turned out, his client was a Somnambulist. A Somnambulist is a person that is so suggestible that it only takes a minute or two for them to go into a deep state of hypnosis. They account for about 7% of the population. Somnambulists are the people you see in the Hypnotist shows.

Somnambulists also have a greater chance of having phobias because their minds are more suggestible than the rest of the population. Haven't you noticed in those shows that 20 people go up on stage to be hypnotized, and all but a few get sent back to their seats? That is because the Hypnotist only uses Somnambulists in his show.

So the challenge was on. Since the client was a Somnambulist it was easy for my colleague to quickly put the man in a deep trance. The Hypnotist took a pencil from his desk and told the client that the pencil was a lit cigarette. He took the client's hand and touched the imagined lit cigarette against the client's palm. The client jumped away as if in pain.

In the state of Hypnosis, this man was so suggestible that when the therapist touched his palm with the pencil, but telling the man that it was a smoldering cigarette, the man felt the pain. His mind believed it so much that it created a burn mark on his palm. You see how powerful the mind is.

Let's get back to the man with the pain is his leg. Dr. Weiss hypnotized his client and had him go back to his childhood to see if his subconscious could recall a time when some kind of trauma happened to his leg. He couldn't recall anything. He kept taking him further and further back into his youth, at one year old, still nothing.

Then Dr. Weiss told the client, "I want you to go back even further in time." A few moments later, his client started to move frantically in his chair. Dr. Weiss quickly took him out of hypnosis. When the man had calmed Dr. Weiss asked him what had happened.

The client with a confused look in his eyes said. I was a soldier, and I was in a trench. It looked like the kind they show in the World War 1 movies. I was fighting a German soldier. I could tell he was German because of his uniform. We were fighting to the death. I felt him stab me with his bayonet in my left leg. At that moment, you brought me out of the trance. Dr. Weiss was amazed. Nothing like this had ever happened in his practice before.

Over the next weeks, Dr. Weiss thought about this experience over and over. He had heard about reincarnation and was not a believer at all. A few weeks later his client dropped by, and showed him he was cured. He no longer walked with a limp or had any pain in his leg. They discussed the experience again, but both of them thought it couldn't be reincarnation. There had to be some other explanation. All that the client knew was that what he experienced in hypnosis took away the pain in his leg.

Still not believing that the cause of some peoples phobias came from past lives, Dr. Weiss continued to use hypnosis to have his clients imagine themselves in previous lives. The same thing kept happening; they would go into a trance and experience an incident that would link the problem they were having in this life, to that lifetime. That would result in the cure for their current problem.

Case History

Past Life Trauma

Issue: Fear of Large Bodies of Water

Ever since, she could remember, this woman had a fear of Large Bodies of water. She was OK around rivers or swimming pools. However, she did refuse to learn to swim. Anytime she would get near a lake or large pond; she would have panic attacks. In previous sessions, they had ruled out that her fear was coming from anything in this lifetime, so they decided that, in her next session, they would try past life regression.

The next week during her session they talked about reincarnation. The client said that she was "on the fence" about past lives, but since nothing they did had worked so far in removing her phobia, she was willing to try a different approach.

In hypnosis, the therapist suggested she go back to a time before this life, back to a time when an incident happened that is now causing her to fear large bodies of water. Within a few minutes, the client started to cry, and then she started to panic. The hypnotist used a technique to calm her down while she was in hypnosis. He told her that she would stop experiencing this event in first person. Instead, she would see what was happening on a movie screen. That calmed her down immediately. In the state of hypnosis, she was now sitting in a theatre and comfortably watching this past life scene on the movie screen. Here is what she saw.

She was in what she described as a Model T, one of the first cars ever built. It was a new car, and her boyfriend had taken her for a ride to a nearby lake. They parked on the edge of the lake, and doing as young lovers do, started making out.

In her passion, her leg hit the emergency brake, causing it to release. The car rolled into the lake and started to submerge. Her boyfriend said, "Don't worry the windows are closed. We will just roll them down and swim away." Now they were under the water, and water was rushing into the car. They tried to roll down the windows, but couldn't. She saw herself screaming in fear. She knew it was all her fault. It was a horrible scene. They both drowned.

Even seeing this on the screen, she was visibly shaken and had begun to cry. The hypnotist calmed her down, explaining that she was OK. He told her that what she just saw was something that happened a long time ago. It was not happening to her now. When she was calm, the therapist brought her out of hypnosis.

In the next session, the client told him that her fear of water had totally gone away. She had her husband take her for the weekend to Lake Michigan, a few hours from her home. For the first time that she could remember she was able to sit comfortably and enjoy the beauty of a lake.

If this phenomena only happened once you could dismiss it as fantasy, but as Doctor Weiss discovered it happened thousands and thousands of times. The same scenario, a client comes in with a fear or phobia, and they try everything they can to find the cause and remove the fear, but to no avail. Then they try past life recall. The client sees a traumatic experience that they had in that lifetime. They come out of hypnosis, and immediately or within a short time, their phobia has disappeared.

The interesting thing is that, even if the person who had what appeared to be a recall from a past life didn't believe in reincarnation, the fear and trauma in their current life would still go away.

Whether you believe in past lives or not, I would hope that you would keep an open mind. After all, the reason for reading this book and learning all this is to help you get rid of your phobias. If nothing else works, you might give Past Life Regression a try.

The good news is that most phobias can be removed by using EFT, a technique that you are about to learn. And the other good news is that, you can use this skill on yourself, and have the same results that you would get with a therapist.

In a minute, you will be reading a long list of phobias. Is yours on the list? You will see that, as human beings, we are afraid of about everything. You will laugh out loud at some of the phobias that people have. Just remember that if you are the one with the silly phobia, it is no laughing matter.

Chapter 5: How Many Phobias are There?

"What we fear comes to pass more speedily than what we hope."

---- Publilius Syrus - Moral Sayings (1st C B.C.)

The phobias are listed in alphabetical order. When you find yours, write down the medical term. You will now have a fancy name for your phobia. If you can't find yours, please email me, and I will add it to the list.

A-

Ablutophobia- Fear of washing or bathing.

Acarophobia- Fear of itching or of the insects that cause itching.

Acerophobia- Fear of sourness.

Achluophobia- Fear of darkness.

Acousticophobia- Fear of noise.

Acrophobia- Fear of heights.

Aerophobia- Fear of drafts, air swallowing, or airborne noxious substances.

Aeroacrophobia- Fear of open high places.

Aeronausiphobia- Fear of vomiting secondary to airsickness.

Agateophobia- Fear of insanity.

Agliophobia- Fear of pain.

Agoraphobia- Fear of open spaces or of being in crowded, public places like markets. Fear of leaving a safe place.

Agraphobia- Fear of sexual abuse.

Agrizoophobia- Fear of wild animals.

Agyrophobia- Fear of streets or crossing the street.

Aichmophobia- Fear of needles or pointed objects.

Ailurophobia- Fear of cats.

Albuminurophobia- Fear of kidney disease.

Alektorophobia- Fear of chickens.

Algophobia- Fear of pain.

Alliumphobia- Fear of garlic.

Allodoxaphobia- Fear of opinions.

Altophobia- Fear of heights.

Amathophobia- Fear of dust.

Amaxophobia- Fear of riding in a car.

Ambulophobia- Fear of walking.

Amnesiphobia- Fear of amnesia.

Amychophobia- Fear of scratches or being scratched.

Anablephobia- Fear of looking up.

Ancraophobia- Fear of wind. (Anemophobia)

Androphobia- Fear of men.

Anemophobia- Fear of air drafts or wind. (Ancraophobia)

Anginophobia- Fear of angina, choking, or narrowness.

Anglophobia- Fear of England or English culture, etc.

Angrophobia - Fear of anger or of becoming angry.

Ankylophobia- Fear of immobility of a joint.

Anthrophobia or Anthophobia- Fear of flowers.

Anthropophobia- Fear of people or society.

Antlophobia- Fear of floods.

Anuptaphobia- Fear of staying single.

Apeirophobia- Fear of infinity.

Aphenphosmphobia- Fear of being touched. (Haphephobia)

Apiphobia- Fear of bees.

Apotemnophobia- Fear of persons with amputations.

Arachibutyrophobia- Fear of peanut butter sticking to the roof of the mouth.

Arachnephobia or Arachnophobia- Fear of spiders.

Arithmophobia- Fear of numbers.

Arrhenphobia- Fear of men.

Arsonphobia- Fear of fire.

Asthenophobia- Fear of fainting or weakness.

Astraphobia or Astrapophobia- Fear of thunder and lightning.(Ceraunophobia, Keraunophobia)

Astrophobia- Fear of stars or celestial space.

Asymmetriphobia- Fear of asymmetrical things.

Ataxiophobia- Fear of ataxia. (muscular incoordination)

Ataxophobia- Fear of disorder or untidiness.

Atelophobia- Fear of imperfection.

Atephobia- Fear of ruin or ruins.

Athazagoraphobia- Fear of being forgotten or ignored or forgetting.

Atomosophobia- Fear of atomic explosions.

Atychiphobia- Fear of failure.

Aulophobia- Fear of flutes.

Aurophobia- Fear of gold.

Auroraphobia- Fear of Northern lights.

Autodysomophobia- Fear of one that has a vile odor.

Automatonophobia- Fear of ventriloquist's dummies, animatronic creatures, waxes statues - anything that falsely represents a sentient being.

Automysophobia- Fear of being dirty.

Autophobia- Fear of being alone or of oneself.

Aviophobia or Aviatophobia- Fear of flying.

B-

Bacillophobia- Fear of microbes.

Bacteriophobia- Fear of bacteria.

Ballistophobia- Fear of missiles or bullets.

Bolshephobia- Fear of Bolsheviks.

Barophobia- Fear of gravity.

Basophobia or Basiphobia- Inability to stand. Fear of walking or falling.

Bathmophobia- Fear of stairs or steep slopes.

Bathophobia- Fear of depth.

Batophobia- Fear of heights or being close to high buildings.

Batrachophobia- Fear of amphibians, such as frogs, newts, salamanders, etc.

Belonephobia- Fear of pins and needles. (Aichmophobia)

Bibliophobia- Fear of books.

Blennophobia- Fear of slime.

Bogyphobia- Fear of bogeys or the bogeyman.

Botanophobia- Fear of plants.

Bromidrosiphobia or Bromidrophobia- Fear of body smells.

Brontophobia- Fear of thunder and lightning.

Bufonophobia- Fear of toads.

C-

Cacophobia- Fear of ugliness.

Cainophobia or Cainotophobia- Fear of newness, novelty.

Caligynephobia- Fear of beautiful women.

Cancerophobia or Carcinophobia- Fear of cancer.

Cardiophobia- Fear of the heart.

Carnophobia- Fear of meat.

Catagelophobia- Fear of being ridiculed.

Catapedaphobia- Fear of jumping from high and low places.

Cathisophobia- Fear of sitting.

Catoptrophobia- Fear of mirrors.

Cenophobia or Centophobia- Fear of new things or ideas.

Ceraunophobia or Keraunophobia- Fear of thunder and lightning.(Astraphobia, Astrapophobia)

Chaetophobia- Fear of hair.

Cheimaphobia or Cheimatophobia- Fear of cold.(Frigophobia, Psychophobia)

Chemophobia- Fear of chemicals or working with chemicals.

Cherophobia- Fear of gaiety.

Chionophobia- Fear of snow.

Chiraptophobia- Fear of being touched.

Chirophobia- Fear of hands.

Chiroptophobia- Fear of bats.

Cholerophobia- Fear of anger or the fear of cholera.

Chorophobia- Fear of dancing.

Chrometophobia or Chrematophobia- Fear of money.

Chromophobia or Chromatophobia- Fear of colors.

Chronophobia- Fear of time.

Chronomentrophobia- Fear of clocks.

Cibophobia- Fear of food.(Sitophobia, Sitiophobia)

Claustrophobia- Fear of confined spaces.

Cleithrophobia or Cleisiophobia- Fear of being locked in an enclosed place.

Cleptophobia- Fear of stealing.

Climacophobia- Fear of stairs, climbing, or of falling downstairs.

Clinophobia- Fear of going to bed.

Clithrophobia or Cleithrophobia- Fear of being enclosed.

Cnidophobia- Fear of stings.

Cometophobia- Fear of comets.

Coimetrophobia- Fear of cemeteries.

Coitophobia- Fear of coitus.

Contreltophobia- Fear of sexual abuse.

Coprastasophobia- Fear of constipation.

Coprophobia- Fear of feces.

Consecotaleophobia- Fear of chopsticks.

Coulrophobia- Fear of clowns.

Counterphobia- The preference by a phobic for fearful situations.

Cremnophobia- Fear of precipices.

Cryophobia- Fear of extreme cold, ice, or frost.

Crystallophobia- Fear of crystals or glass.

Cyberphobia- Fear of computers or working on a computer.

Cyclophobia- Fear of bicycles.

Cymophobia or Kymophobia- Fear of waves or wave like motions.

Cynophobia- Fear of dogs or rabies.

Cypridophobia or Cypriphobia or Cyprianophobia or Cyprinophobia - Fear of prostitutes or venereal disease.

D

Decidophobia- Fear of making decisions.

Defecaloesiophobia- Fear of painful bowels movements.

Deipnophobia- Fear of dining or dinner conversations.

Dementophobia- Fear of insanity.

Demonophobia or Daemonophobia- Fear of demons.

Demophobia- Fear of crowds. (Agoraphobia)

Dendrophobia- Fear of trees.

Dentophobia- Fear of dentists.

Dermatophobia- Fear of skin lesions.

Dermatosiophobia or Dermatophobia or Dermatopathophobia- Fear of skin disease.

Dextrophobia- Fear of objects at the right side of the body.

Diabetophobia- Fear of diabetes.

Didaskaleinophobia- Fear of going to school.

Dikephobia- Fear of justice.

Dinophobia- Fear of dizziness or whirlpools.

Diplophobia- Fear of double vision.

Dipsophobia- Fear of drinking.

Dishabiliophobia- Fear of undressing in front of someone.

Disposophobia- Fear of throwing stuff out. Hoarding.

Domatophobia- Fear of houses or being in a house.(Eicophobia, Oikophobia)

Doraphobia- Fear of fur or skins of animals.

Doxophobia- Fear of expressing opinions or of receiving praise.

Dromophobia- Fear of crossing streets.

Dutchphobia- Fear of the Dutch.

Dysmorphophobia- Fear of deformity.

Dystychiphobia- Fear of accidents.

E

Ecclesiophobia- Fear of church.

Ecophobia- Fear of home.

Eicophobia- Fear of home
surroundings.(Domatophobia, Oikophobia)

Eisoptrophobia- Fear of mirrors or of seeing
oneself in a mirror.

Electrophobia- Fear of electricity.

Eleutherophobia- Fear of freedom.

Elurophobia- Fear of cats. (Ailurophobia)

Emetophobia- Fear of vomiting.

Enetophobia- Fear of pins.

Enochlophobia- Fear of crowds.

Enosiophobia or Enissophobia- Fear of having committed an unpardonable sin or of criticism.

Entomophobia- Fear of insects.

Eosophobia- Fear of dawn or daylight.

Ephebiphobia- Fear of teenagers.

Epistaxiophobia- Fear of nosebleeds.

Epistemophobia- Fear of knowledge.

Equinophobia- Fear of horses.

Eremophobia- Fear of being oneself or of loneliness.

Ereuthrophobia- Fear of blushing.

Ergasiophobia- 1) Fear of work or functioning. 2) Surgeon's fear of operating.

Ergophobia- Fear of work.

Erotophobia- Fear of sexual love or sexual questions.

Euphobia- Fear of hearing good news.

Eurotophobia- Fear of female genitalia.

Erythrophobia or Erytophobia or Ereuthophobia- 1) Fear of redlights. 2) Blushing. 3) Red.

F

Febriphobia or Fibriphobia or Fibriophobia- Fear of fever.

Felinophobia- Fear of cats. (Ailurophobia, Elurophobia, Galeophobia, Gatophobia)

Francophobia- Fear of France or French culture. (Gallophobia, Galiophobia)

Frigophobia- Fear of cold or cold things.(Cheimaphobia, Cheimatophobia, Psychrophobia)

G

Galeophobia or Gatophobia- Fear of cats.

Gallophobia or Galiophobia- Fear France or French culture. (Francophobia)

Gamophobia- Fear of marriage.

Geliophobia- Fear of laughter.

Gelotophobia- Fear of being laughed at.

Geniophobia- Fear of chins.

Genophobia- Fear of sex.

Genuphobia- Fear of knees.

Gephyrophobia or Gephydrophobia or Gephysrophobia- Fear of crossing bridges.

Germanophobia- Fear of Germany or German culture.

Gerascophobia- Fear of growing old.

Gerontophobia- Fear of old people or of growing old.

Geumaphobia or Geumophobia- Fear of taste.

Glossophobia- Fear of speaking in public or of trying to speak.

Gnosiophobia- Fear of knowledge.

Graphophobia- Fear of writing or handwriting.

Gymnophobia- Fear of nudity.

Gynephobia or Gynophobia- Fear of women.

H-

Hadephobia- Fear of hell.

Hagiophobia- Fear of saints or holy things.

Hamartophobia- Fear of sinning.

Haphephobia or Haptephobia- Fear of being touched.

Harpaxophobia- Fear of being robbed.

Hedonophobia- Fear of feeling pleasure.

Heliophobia- Fear of the sun.

Hellenologophobia- Fear of Greek terms or complex scientific terminology.

Helminthophobia- Fear of being infested with worms.

Hemophobia or Hemaphobia or Hematophobia- Fear of blood.

Heresyphobia or Hereiophobia- Fear of challenges to official doctrine or of radical deviation.

Herpetophobia- Fear of reptiles or creepy, crawly things.

Heterophobia- Fear of the opposite sex. (Sexophobia)

Hexakosioihexekontahexaphobia- Fear of the number 666.

Hierophobia- Fear of priests or sacred things.

Hippophobia- Fear of horses.

Hippopotomonstrosesquipedaliophobia- Fear of long words.

Hobophobia- Fear of bums or beggars.

Hodophobia- Fear of road travel.

Hormephobia- Fear of shock.

Homichlophobia- Fear of fog.

Homilophobia- Fear of sermons.

Hominophobia- Fear of men.

Homophobia- Fear of sameness, monotony or of homosexuality or of becoming homosexual.

Hoplophobia- Fear of firearms.

Hydrargyophobia- Fear of mercurial medicines.

Hydrophobia- Fear of water or of rabies.

Hydrophobophobia- Fear of rabies.

Hyelophobia or Hyalophobia- Fear of glass.

Hygrophobia- Fear of liquids, dampness, or moisture.

Hylephobia- Fear of materialism or the fear of epilepsy.

Hylophobia- Fear of forests.

Hypengyophobia or Hypegiaphobia- Fear of responsibility.

Hypnophobia- Fear of sleep or of being hypnotized.

Hypsiphobia- Fear of height.

I-

Iatrophobia- Fear of going to the doctor or of doctors.

Ichthyophobia- Fear of fish.

Ideophobia- Fear of ideas.

Illyngophobia- Fear of vertigo or feeling dizzy when looking down.

Iophobia- Fear of poison.

Insectophobia - Fear of insects.

Isolophobia- Fear of solitude, being alone.

Isopterophobia- Fear of termites, insects that eat wood.

Ithyphallophobia- Fear of seeing, thinking about or having an erect penis.

J-

Japanophobia- Fear of Japanese.

Judeophobia- Fear of Jews.

K-

Kainolophobia or Kainophobia- Fear of anything new, novelty.

Kakorrhaphiophobia- Fear of failure or defeat.

Katagelophobia- Fear of ridicule.

Kathisophobia- Fear of sitting down.

Katsaridaphobia- Fear of cockroaches.

Kenophobia- Fear of voids or empty spaces.

Keraunophobia or Ceraunophobia- Fear of thunder and lightning.(Astraphobia, Astrapophobia)

Kinetophobia or Kinesophobia- Fear of movement or motion.

Kleptophobia- Fear of stealing.

Koinoniphobia- Fear of rooms.

Kolpophobia- Fear of genitals, particularly female.

Kopophobia- Fear of fatigue.

Koniophobia- Fear of dust. (Amathophobia)

Kosmikophobia- Fear of cosmic phenomenon.

Kymophobia- Fear of waves. (Cymophobia)

Kynophobia- Fear of rabies.

Kyphophobia- Fear of stooping.

L-

Lachanophobia- Fear of vegetables.

Laliophobia or Lalophobia- Fear of speaking.

Leprophobia or Lepraphobia- Fear of leprosy.

Leukophobia- Fear of the color white.

Levophobia- Fear of things to the left side of the body.

Ligyrophobia- Fear of loud noises.

Lilapsophobia- Fear of tornadoes and hurricanes.

Limnophobia- Fear of lakes.

Linonophobia- Fear of string.

Liticaphobia- Fear of lawsuits.

Lockiophobia- Fear of childbirth.

Logizomechanophobia- Fear of computers.

Logophobia- Fear of words.

Luiphobia- Fear of lues, syphillis.

Lutraphobia- Fear of otters.

Lygophobia- Fear of darkness.

Lyssophobia- Fear of rabies or of becoming mad.

M-

Macrophobia- Fear of long waits.

Mageirocophobia- Fear of cooking.

Maieusiophobia- Fear of childbirth.

Malaxophobia- Fear of love play.
(Sarmassophobia)

Maniaphobia- Fear of insanity.

Mastigophobia- Fear of punishment.

Mechanophobia- Fear of machines.

Medomalacuphobia- Fear of losing an erection.

Medorthophobia- Fear of an erect penis.

Megalophobia- Fear of large things.

Melissophobia- Fear of bees.

Melanophobia- Fear of the color black.

Melophobia- Fear or hatred of music.

Meningitophobia- Fear of brain disease.

Menophobia- Fear of menstruation.

Merinthophobia- Fear of being bound or tied up.

Metallophobia- Fear of metal.

Metathesiophobia- Fear of changes.

Meteorophobia- Fear of meteors.

Methyphobia- Fear of alcohol.

Metrophobia- Fear or hatred of poetry.

Microbiophobia- Fear of microbes. (Bacillophobia)

Microphobia- Fear of small things.

Misophobia or Mysophobia- Fear of being contaminated with dirt or germs.

Mnemophobia- Fear of memories.

Molysmophobia or Molysomophobia- Fear of dirt or contamination.

Monophobia- Fear of solitude or being alone.

Monopathophobia- Fear of definite disease.

Motorphobia- Fear of automobiles.

Mottephobia- Fear of moths.

Musophobia or Muriphobia- Fear of mice.

Mycophobia- Fear or aversion to mushrooms.

Mycrophobia- Fear of small things.

Myctophobia- Fear of darkness.

Myrmecophobia- Fear of ants.

Mythophobia- Fear of myths or stories or false statements.

Myxophobia- Fear of slime. (Blennophobia)

N

Nebulaphobia- Fear of fog. (Homichlophobia)

Necrophobia- Fear of death or dead things.

Nelophobia- Fear of glass.

Neopharmaphobia- Fear of new drugs.

Neophobia- Fear of anything new.

Nephophobia- Fear of clouds.

Noctiphobia- Fear of the night.

Nomatophobia- Fear of names.

Nosocomephobia- Fear of hospitals.

Nosophobia or Nosemaphobia- Fear of becoming ill.

Nostophobia- Fear of returning home.

Novercaphobia- Fear of your step-mother.

Nucleomituphobia- Fear of nuclear weapons.

Nudophobia- Fear of nudity.

Numerophobia- Fear of numbers.

Nyctohylophobia- Fear of dark wooded areas or of forests at night

Nyctophobia- Fear of the dark or of night.

O-

Obesophobia- Fear of gaining weight.(Pocrescophobia)

Ochlophobia- Fear of crowds or mobs.

Ochophobia- Fear of vehicles.

Octophobia - Fear of the figure 8.

Odontophobia- Fear of teeth or dental surgery.

Odynophobia or Odynephobia- Fear of pain.
(Algophobia)

Oenophobia- Fear of wines.

Oikophobia- Fear of home surroundings,
house.(Domatophobia, Eicophobia)

Olfactophobia- Fear of smells.

Ombrophobia- Fear of rain or of being rained on.

Ommetaphobia or Ommatophobia- Fear of eyes.

Omphalophobia- Fear of belly buttons.

Oneirophobia- Fear of dreams.

Oneirogmophobia- Fear of wet dreams.

Onomatophobia- Fear of hearing a certain word or of names.

Ophidiophobia- Fear of snakes. (Snakephobia)

Ophthalmophobia- Fear of being stared at.

Opiophobia- Fear medical doctor's experience of prescribing needed pain medications for patients.

Optophobia- Fear of opening one's eyes.

Ornithophobia- Fear of birds.

Orthophobia- Fear of property.

Osmophobia or Osphresiophobia- Fear of smells or odors.

Ostraconophobia- Fear of shellfish.

Ouranophobia or Uranophobia- Fear of heaven.

P

Pagophobia- Fear of ice or frost.

Panthophobia- Fear of suffering and disease.

Panophobia or Pantophobia- Fear of everything.

Papaphobia- Fear of the Pope.

Papyrophobia- Fear of paper.

Paralipophobia- Fear of neglecting duty or responsibility.

Paraphobia- Fear of sexual perversion.

Parasitophobia- Fear of parasites.

Paraskavedekatriaphobia- Fear of Friday the 13th.

Parthenophobia- Fear of virgins or young girls.

Pathophobia- Fear of disease.

Patroiophobia- Fear of heredity.

Parturiphobia- Fear of childbirth.

Peccatophobia- Fear of sinning or imaginary crimes.

Pediculophobia- Fear of lice.

Pediophobia- Fear of dolls.

Pedophobia- Fear of children.

Peladophobia- Fear of bald people.

Pellagrophobia- Fear of pellagra.

Peniaphobia- Fear of poverty.

Pentheraphobia- Fear of mother-in-law. Novercaphobia)

Phagophobia- Fear of swallowing or of eating or of being eaten.

Phalacrophobia- Fear of becoming bald.

Phallophobia- Fear of a penis, esp erect.

Pharmacophobia- Fear of taking medicine.

Phasmophobia- Fear of ghosts.

Phengophobia- Fear of daylight or sunshine.

Philemaphobia or Philematophobia- Fear of kissing.

Philophobia- Fear of falling in love or being in love.

Philosophobia- Fear of philosophy.

Phobophobia- Fear of phobias.

Photoaugliaphobia- Fear of glaring lights.

Photophobia- Fear of light.

Phonophobia- Fear of noises or voices or one's own voice; of telephones.

Phronemophobia- Fear of thinking.

Phthiriophobia- Fear of lice. (Pediculophobia)

Phthisiophobia- Fear of tuberculosis.

Placophobia- Fear of tombstones.

Plutophobia- Fear of wealth.

Pluviophobia- Fear of rain or of being rained on.

Pneumatiphobia- Fear of spirits.

Pnigophobia or Pnigerophobia- Fear of choking of being smothered.

Pocrescophobia- Fear of gaining weight. Obesophobia)

Pogonophobia- Fear of beards.

Poliosophobia- Fear of contracting poliomyelitis.

Politicophobia- Fear or abnormal dislike of politicians.

Polyphobia- Fear of many things.

Poinephobia- Fear of punishment.

Ponophobia- Fear of overworking or of pain.

Porphyrophobia- Fear of the color purple.

Potamophobia- Fear of rivers or running water.

Potophobia- Fear of alcohol.

Pharmacophobia- Fear of drugs.

Proctophobia- Fear of rectums.

Prosophobia- Fear of progress.

Psellismophobia- Fear of stuttering.

Psychophobia- Fear of mind.

Psychrophobia- Fear of cold.

Pteromerhanophobia- Fear of flying.

Pteronophobia- Fear of being tickled by feathers.

Pupaphobia - Fear of puppets.

Pyrexiophobia- Fear of Fever.

Pyrophobia- Fear of fire.

Q-

R-

Radiophobia- Fear of radiation, x-rays.

Ranidaphobia- Fear of frogs.

Rectophobia- Fear of rectum or rectal diseases.

Rhabdophobia- Fear of being severely punished or beaten by a rod, or of being severely criticized. Also, fear of magic.(wand)

Rhypophobia- Fear of defecation.

Rhytiphobia- Fear of getting wrinkles.

Rupophobia- Fear of dirt.

Russophobia- Fear of Russians.

S-

Samhainophobia: Fear of Halloween.

Sarmassophobia- Fear of love play. (Malaxophobia)

Satanophobia- Fear of Satan.

Scabiophobia- Fear of scabies.

Scatophobia- Fear of fecal matter.

Scelerophibia- Fear of bad men, burglars.

Sciophobia Sciaphobia- Fear of shadows.

Scoleciphobia- Fear of worms.

Scolionophobia- Fear of school.

Scopophobia or Scoptophobia- Fear of being seen or stared at.

Scotomaphobia- Fear of blindness in visual field.

Scotophobia- Fear of darkness. (Achluophobia)

Scriptophobia- Fear of writing in public.

Selachophobia- Fear of sharks.

Selaphobia- Fear of light flashes.

Selenophobia- Fear of the moon.

Seplophobia- Fear of decaying matter.

Sesquipedalophobia- Fear of long words.

Sexophobia- Fear of the opposite sex.
Heterophobia)

Siderodromophobia- Fear of trains, railroads, or
train travel.

Siderophobia- Fear of stars.

Sinistrophobia- Fear of things to the left or left-
handed.

Sinophobia- Fear of Chinese, Chinese culture.

Sitophobia or Sitiophobia- Fear of food or eating. (Cibophobia)

Snakephobia- Fear of snakes. (Ophidiophobia)

Soceraphobia- Fear of parents-in-law.

Social Phobia- Fear of being evaluated negatively in social situations.

Sociophobia- Fear of society or people in general.

Somniphobia- Fear of sleep.

Sophophobia- Fear of learning.

Soteriophobia - Fear of dependence on others.

Spacephobia- Fear of outer space.

Spectrophobia- Fear of specters or ghosts.

Spermatophobia or Spermophobia- Fear of germs.

Spheksophobia- Fear of wasps.

Stasibasiphobia or Stasiphobia- Fear of standing or walking. (Ambulophobia)

Staurophobia- Fear of crosses or the crucifix.

Stenophobia- Fear of narrow things or places.

Stygiophobia or Stigiophobia- Fear of hell.

Suriphobia- Fear of mice.

Symbolophobia- Fear of symbolism.

Symmetrophobia- Fear of symmetry.

Syngenesophobia- Fear of relatives.

Syphilophobia- Fear of syphilis.

T-

Tachophobia- Fear of speed.

Taeniophobia or Teniophobia- Fear of tapeworms.

Taphephobia Taphophobia- Fear of being buried alive or of cemeteries.

Tapinophobia- Fear of being contagious.

Taurophobia- Fear of bulls.

Technophobia- Fear of technology.

Teleophobia- 1) Fear of definite plans. 2) Religious ceremony.

Telephonophobia- Fear of telephones.

Teratophobia- Fear of bearing a deformed child or fear of monsters or deformed people.

Testophobia- Fear of taking tests.

Tetanophobia- Fear of lockjaw, tetanus.

Teutophobia- Fear of German or German things.

Textophobia- Fear of certain fabrics.

Thaasophobia- Fear of sitting.

Thalassophobia- Fear of the sea.

Thanatophobia or Thantophobia- Fear of death or dying.

Theatrophobia- Fear of theatres.

Theologicophobia- Fear of theology.

Theophobia- Fear of gods or religion.

Thermophobia- Fear of heat.

Tocophobia- Fear of pregnancy or childbirth.

Tomophobia- Fear of surgical operations.

Tonitrophobia- Fear of thunder.

Topophobia- Fear of certain places or situations, such as stage fright.

Toxiphobia or Toxophobia or Toxicophobia- Fear of poison or of being accidently poisoned.

Traumatophobia- Fear of injury.

Tremophobia- Fear of trembling.

Trichinophobia- Fear of trichinosis.

Trichopathophobia or Trichophobia- Fear of hair. (Chaetophobia, Hypertrichophobia)

Triskaidekaphobia- Fear of the number 13.

Tropophobia- Fear of moving or making changes.

Trypanophobia- Fear of injections.

Tuberculophobia- Fear of tuberculosis.

Tyrannophobia- Fear of tyrants.

U-

Uranophobia or Ouranophobia- Fear of heaven.

Urophobia- Fear of urine or urinating.

V-

Vaccinophobia- Fear of vaccination.

Venustraphobia- Fear of beautiful women.

Verbophobia- Fear of words.

Verminophobia- Fear of germs.

Vestiphobia- Fear of clothing.

Virginitiphobia- Fear of rape.

Vitricophobia- Fear of step-father.

W-

Walloonphobia- Fear of the Walloons.

Wiccaphobia: Fear of witches and witchcraft.

X-

Xanthophobia- Fear of the color yellow or the word yellow.

Xenoglossophobia- Fear of foreign languages.

Xenophobia- Fear of strangers or foreigners.

Xerophobia- Fear of dryness.

Xylophobia- 1) Fear of wooden objects. 2) Forests.

Xyrophobia-Fear of razors.

Y-

Z-

Zelophobia- Fear of jealousy.

Zeusophobia- Fear of God or gods.

Zemmiphobia- Fear of the great mole rat.

Zoophobia- Fear of animals.

There were almost 500 phobias listed above. Can you see why I am a very busy therapist? Did you find yours? If so, what was the fancy name for it? As I said, if you didn't find yours, email me and I will put it in the next edition of this book.

Now that, you know you are not alone and that millions around the world have some sort of phobia, it is time to learn about the tool I will teach you to take your phobia away. The procedure you will learn as I mentioned earlier is called EFT or Emotional Freedom Technique.

Taking Away a Phobia at a Bar

Besides being a Hypnotherapist and EFT Practitioner, I am a Hand Writing Analyst. Hand Writing Analysis was part of the curriculum at Hypnotherapy

College. We used it to tell quickly how introvert or extrovert a new client was. Extroverts are usually hypnotized more easily than introverts. Instead of asking 50 questions and it's time for the session to be over, we have them write a few sentences and can tell immediately what Hypnosis techniques will be more successful with them. That way we can get right to work and not waste the client's time or money.

I had been hired by an upscale nightclub in San Bernardino CA to come in one night and do Hand Writing Analysis as entertainment for their patrons. I know that sounds pretty strange, but actually it was quite the experience.

This was on a hot summer night in August, and when we arrived there were already hundreds of people at the club.

I forgot to mention that my girlfriend is a Hypnotherapist and Hand Writing Analyst also. I had called the club and asked if I could bring her along. They said that actually, they would prefer that.

The people were very genuine and kind to us, and they absolutely loved having us analyze their hand writing. One thing that many of them did was write their "y's" with a big loop at the bottom. That indicates a subconscious desire for lots of sex. When we would tell them their writing showed that they were extremely "frisky," we always got a laugh.

That night we met some really nice people. We analyzed the writing of a doctor and his wife, a nurse, a building contractor, some state workers, a fireman, a man who worked for Disney Studios, a couple who were both sheriff's and a cook. The reason I'm telling you this is because of the story of Chris.

Case History

Chris

Issue: Fear of Ketchup

That night at the club I met a great guy and his girlfriend. He worked for the police department as a CSI (crime scene investigator). While I was analyzing his handwriting, I mentioned about being a Hypnotherapist, and that I specialized in helping people rid themselves of their fears and phobias. His girlfriend spoke up and said, in a teasing way, Chris, "maybe he can help you get rid of your big fear." I'm thinking, this guy is CSI, he is around dead bodies all the time, and I bet that his fear or phobia is work related.

I said to Chris, "What is your fear?" He hesitated for a minute. His girlfriend was giving him a strange look as if she knew it was going to be hard for him to tell me what it was. He was still having trouble saying what it was and then his girlfriend just blurts it out, "He's afraid of Ketchup." I laughed out loud thinking it was a joke, but then noticed the look on his face. Then I started feeling bad that I laughed. Chris was,"really" afraid of Ketchup.

I immediately apologized. He was looking embarrassed. I couldn't wrap my mind around that here was this tall, well built, macho policeman who investigates crime scenes; and he's afraid of what? Then it came to me. Ketchup, it looks like blood. That has to be it.

I asked him about the connection. Are you afraid of blood? He said, " no, not at all. I'm around blood all the time at crime scenes and it never bothers me." Well if it is not the obvious, what could it be? I really switched into "therapist mode" and realized the first thing I needed to establish was he experiencing a fear or was it a phobia. I asked him if there was an incident in his life that he could remember that would have made him afraid of ketchup. There were none that he could remember.

I looked at my watch and realized we were done with entertaining in another hour. I told him that if he wanted me to help eliminate his fear I would help him before we left. I told him I was willing to do it for free. He said he would think about it.

We finished our gig, and were getting ready to leave when he walked up to me and asked if I was still willing to help him. He wanted to give it a try. I told him and his girlfriend to follow me outside to the patio area where it was quiet. I sat him down and began the process.

Usually when I work with my clients, I show them a 20 minute video tape that explains how this EFT (tapping) works. They actually see this technique work on people that have some really severe issues. It helps them make the paradigm shift into a new way of looking at things. As I said earlier in this book, one nice thing about EFT is that it works for you whether you believe it will or not.

His girlfriend said it really bothered her that if she ate something with ketchup on it, he wouldn't touch her for the rest of the night. If they went into a coffee shop and there was ketchup on the table, he would ask the waitress to remove it before he sat down. This was embarrassing for her and for him, but he had to do this. His coworkers would tease him by throwing packets of ketchup at him. One time they put a bunch of ketchup in his desk drawer and watched as he jumped away from his desk as if he had seen a snake. The funny thing is he probably would not have been afraid of a snake.

I now knew that this was a serious problem for Chris. It was affecting his relationship with his girlfriend and his self esteem was taking a hit from all the ridicule from his coworkers. It was time to show him the magic of EFT.

First I had him close his eyes. I wanted to get a reading on how afraid of ketchup he was. I asked him to imagine that someone put a whole plate of ketchup in his hands. As he imagined holding the Ketchup, he started visibly shaking. His face became distorted as he grimaced. I then told him to imagine a scale with numbers from 1 to 10 and to watch the needle as it rose on the scale. I asked him what number the needle was pointing to. I could tell by his body language that it was high. "A ten", he says.

Since we didn't have time to teach him how to tap himself, I did the tapping for him.

I did one round, and when we tested, his fear on his scale went to an 8. We did another round it went to 5. Then a third round and all of a sudden there was calm in his face. He said it felt as if his fear was only at a 1 or 2.

While I was doing the tapping, my girlfriend had gone to the kitchen and poured a half of a bottle of ketchup on a plate, and here she was. I had him open his eyes and hold out his hands and then instructed my girlfriend to put the plate of gooey red ketchup in his hands. For an instant he flinched, and then the miracle happened. He held the plate of ketchup and just stared at it. The look on his face was priceless as it always is when a phobia just vanishes. Your conscience mind is saying, "No, this can't be," but in reality it is. The fear or phobia has just vanished.

He continued to stare at the ketchup for minutes and then just smiled. He looked at me and said this is so weird. My mind is telling me I should be afraid of this, but I'm not. I still don't want to touch it or eat it, but I am no longer afraid of it.

You should have seen the look on his girlfriends face. She could see his face and body had returned to center. His relief was obvious. She said, "Isn't this going to be a temporary thing? When he wakes up in the morning won't he be afraid all over again?" I told them he had an 80% chance that it was gone for good.

I wondered what the people who walked by us while I was tapping on him must of thought. Here was this guy in a tuxedo tapping all over a man's body with his fingers while the man held a plate of ketchup in his hands. Anyway, my girlfriend and I still remember the night we took away a man's fear of ketchup in a night club at 2am in the morning.

It has been years now, and I still get an occasional email from Chris thanking me for what happened that night. He has referred many other CSI people to me, and I have helped every one of them.

When your emotional scale goes to a ten, it doesn't matter whether you are afraid of ketchup or afraid of snakes, it feels the same. The panic you feel can be just as great. This may sound silly to you unless you are the one with the fear. EFT will work for you no matter what the fear.

Chapter 6: What is EFT?

"Why are we scared to die? Do any of us remember being scared when we were born?"
---- *Trevor Kay*

EFT or Emotional Freedom Technique (also known as "Tapping") is a unique self-healing technique that helps alleviate emotional and physical problems by using key phrases while tapping on the body's acupuncture meridians. Instead of using needles as in acupuncture, you use your fingertips to tap on the various points. For most issues, you only need to learn where nine points are. It is really easy. I have a chart for you coming up to show you where these points are located.

EFT was discovered in the 80's and has finally come into its own. That is mainly due to the growing body of undeniable research done in the last 10 years.

Many of the studies were done at the Harvard Medical School.

One such study done at the university showed that stimulating these meridian points reduced the brains stress and fear response in the part of the brain called the Amygdala.

Another study that was repeated over and over again showed that tapping reduces the stress hormone "cortisol" by an average of 24% in just a few rounds of tapping. That is compared to 0% in traditional psychotherapy.

Dr. Church also created The Stress Project, which teaches tapping to war veterans suffering with PTSD. The results have been astounding: an average 63% decrease in PTSD symptoms after six rounds of tapping. It's mind-blowing and exciting research, which has converted many non-believers along the way.

These studies tell us therapists what we have observed for years in our clients. We see our emotionally stressed out clients return to center in just a few minutes of tapping. We see their phobias disappear right before our eyes.

The reason I am telling you all this is that many of us, including me had to have a paradigm shift in order to grasp the importance of EFT. EFT and other emerging therapies are the HOLY GRAIL in a new age of healing modalities.

Now I want to show you EFT in action. I want you to watch three short videos on YouTube. You will watch miracles happen. If you don't have access to a computer then just read the short description of each video.

Video One

In Rwanda, a team of EFT practitioners did group sessions for hundreds of survivors of the government's massive genocide campaign. The Rwanda government slaughtered over one million people in 100 days leaving untold thousands of orphans. EFT was taught to the surviving children and then they went out and taught other children how to "tap." The incidences of violence in the orphanages were reduced by an astounding 90% the following year. Here is a heart warming video about EFT in Rwanda.

Ctrl + click on the link
http://www.youtube.com/watch?v=Ymp4vbK8O0g

If clicking on the link didn't work, then cut and paste it into your URL. You can also just go to YouTube and type in   *EFT_Rwanda_video on YouTube.*

Video Two

A team of EFT practitioners from France went to Haiti after the devastating earthquake in 2010. They have had tremendous success helping heal the Haitians traumatic wounds. A lot of people had developed phobias of "fear of being in buildings." The video is in French with English subtitles.

Ctrl + click on the link
http://www.youtube.com/watch?v=BFhdLWEjxuQ

If the link above didn't work then go to YouTube and type in

EFT Haiti 2011.

There is now a team of EFT therapists in Sandy Town helping the town heal from the massacre recently.

What I am trying to do for you is to help your logical mind develop a belief in the benefits of EFT. As I said in the introduction, I never became a true believer until I used it on a client for the first time and had immediate results.

Other clients whom I have taught EFT have themselves started teaching it. You will be learning a skill that you will use daily for the rest of your life. Using EFT will vastly improve the quality of your life and those around you.

Video Three

I am going to have you go to the internet and watch a video called "*EFT for War Veterans*." This is a 19 minute video that gives a great overview of EFT and its miraculous powers. You will see 4 veterans with severe PTSD (Post Traumatic Stress Syndrome). They will transform In front of your eyes. You will see them get their lives back.

The negative emotional energy surrounding your phobias and fears will dissolve just like the veterans did.

Go to YouTube and type this in the search box.

EFT for War Veterans   19 min.

That should do it. Here is the link in case you need it.

http://www.youtube.com/watch?v=yHE684m6nIE

You have just seen three videos showing the incredible benefits of EFT. I have told you of the scientific studies showing that EFT is for real. I am hoping you have now begun to see healing in a whole new way.

Now it is time to learn how to tap. No need to stress, as it is very easy to learn.

Chapter 7: The Tapping Points

"Solitude scares me. It makes me think about love, death, and war. I need a distraction from anxious, black thoughts."

---- Brigitte Bardot

Before having your private session, you need to learn this very simple tapping procedure and practice the tapping points. The following chart will familiarize you with the points on your body that you are going to tap in your personal therapy session. There are only nine tapping points to learn. I told you this was easy.

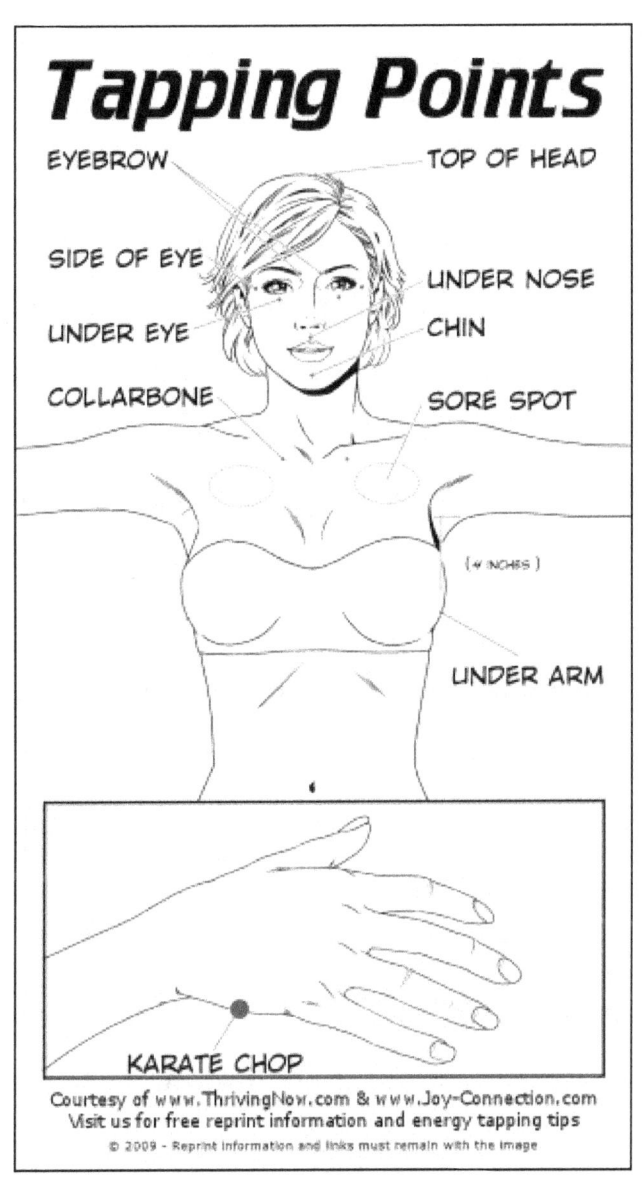

Tapping Points

EYEBROW

TOP OF HEAD

SIDE OF EYE

UNDER NOSE

UNDER EYE

CHIN

COLLARBONE

SORE SPOT

(4 INCHES)

UNDER ARM

KARATE CHOP

Learning the Tapping Points

The points you are about to learn are for what we call "The Short Version" of tapping.

There is a longer version that we use for people on occasion that has additional tapping points, but for the most part the Short Version works the best and is easier to teach. I would say that I use the short version about 80% of the time. I use the longer version of tapping only with really stubborn issues.

In general when tapping, use two or three fingers. That will ensure that you are hitting the point. Tap hard enough to feel it, but not hard enough to be painful. Tap from 6 to 8 times on each point.

You could tap in any order, but for the purposes of learning, it is easier to tap the points from the top of the head down. You will always start at the karate chop point on the side of either hand then go to the crown of the head and work your way down. It doesn't matter if you tap on the right or the left hand. The karate chop point on the left hand goes to the same organs as the karate chop point on the right does. Similarly, the tapping points around the side of the left eye go to the same organs as the same points around the right eye do. The tapping points at the collar bone and under the arm of the left side go to the same organs that the right side points go to. Tap on which side of the body you feel most comfortable with.

Point One: The Karate Chop Point located on the side of each hand

Point Two: Crown of the Head It is the point at the center of your head between your ears, I pat that area with my four fingers to make sure I find the right point.

Point Three: Inner Side of the Eyebrow It is just above the nose.

Point Four: Side of the Eye on the bone bordering the outside corner of the eye

Point Five: Under the Eye On the bone under the eye about 1 inch below your pupil

Point Six: Under the Nose On the small area between the bottom of your nose and the top of your upper lip.

Point Seven: The Cleft of the Chin

Point Eight: Collarbone Point It is at the junction where the sternum (breastbone), collarbone and the first rib meet. To locate it, first place your forefinger on the U-shaped notch at the top of the breastbone (about where a man would knot his tie). From the bottom of the U, move your forefinger down toward the navel 1 inch and then go to the left (or right) 1 inch.

Point Nine : Under the Arm It's on the side of the body, at a point even with the nipple (for men) or in the middle of the bra strap (for women). It is about 4 inches below the armpit.

That is it; you now know the 9 points. You have also watched EFT in action in the videos. When watching the videos you also noticed that while tapping, the clients repeated certain phrases. This is the key to having success with EFT. Next, you will learn what to say while tapping.

Chapter 8: What To Say While Tapping

"Am I afraid of high notes? Of course, I am afraid. What sane man is not?"

---- Luciano Pavarotti

The key to having success with "Tapping" is in understanding that it is a twofold process. The first process is the actual tapping on the body's meridians. The second process is what you say while tapping.

The talking process also has two phases. One is to identify the issue you have. The other part is saying a phrase of self acceptance:

Even though, I have this fear of _____, *I deeply and completely love and accept myself.*

For about 50% of you, what you have just learned is all you will need to know to rid you of your phobia. You will tap on the 9 points while repeating the above phrase and "bingo," you're done. It may take a number of rounds. I find it usually takes from 6 to 8 rounds to get the fear to disappear or lessen to an acceptable level.

In order to gauge the degree of relief from the intensity of your phobia, there are two things you must do before you start tapping. The first thing is to check in to see how high your Emotional Meter goes, and the second is to identify where in your body you feel the fear.

The Mind's Emotional Meter

We all have an imaginary Emotional Meter in our minds. The meter goes from 1-10, 10 being the highest of emotions, 1 being the least. There is a needle, like a speedometer needle that we can see in our minds. The higher the negative emotion, the higher on the meter the needle goes. One of the first things you will do BEFORE you start tapping is to close your eyes and take a minute or two to visualize yourself being in a situation where you are faced with your fear. Really get into it. See how high you can get your fear to go. You will then make note how high on the scale your fear is.

Impromptu Client Session

I had a booth in Balboa Park next to the San Diego Zoo one day. I had my sign out saying that I could get rid of people's phobias in less than an hour. A newlywed couple from Saudi Arabia was visiting the US on their honeymoon. The husband came up to me and said that on their honeymoon he had discovered that his new bride had a huge phobia of insects. She had never told him before getting married about having this fear. He said it was really hard for them to have any fun in the US because they were going to all these outdoor places and she was having panic attacks when seeing any kind of crawling bugs.

I told him not to worry and had his wife sit down in the clients' chair. I had her close her eyes and imagine seeing her inner "Emotional Meter." She could see it and then I asked her where they were staying while in San Diego. She said the Hilton Hotel. I had her imagine sleeping comfortably, feeling the luxurious sheets and soft pillow she was engulfed in. I then had her imagine opening her eyes, and on the pillow about a foot away from her face was an ant. I was not prepared for her response as her emotion skyrocketed to a 10 plus. I had her immediately open her eyes and calmed her down. We all laughed for a moment. Her husband smiled and said, "see what I'm talking about?"

We started the tapping, and after 5 rounds of tapping which took all of 10 minutes, I had her close her eyes and again imagine waking up with an ant on her pillow. This time there was no emotional response. I had her see a whole line of ants crawling on her pillow and no emotional response. I then went for broke and had her visualize that the ants were crawling on her, still no emotional response.

She opened her eyes and was amazed that she no longer felt afraid of bugs. I told her that she had about an 80% chance that she was done with it for good. If some of the fear came back, I showed her how to tap it away quickly. When they returned to Saudi Arabia they emailed me and said that the rest of their honeymoon had been" fear free," and they thanked me again.

When your minds emotional meter gets down to zero or a very low number, it usually means that in a real life setting your fear is going to be gone also.

Where In The Body Do You Feel The Fear?

When you have identified how high your fear is on your Emotional Meter, then find out where in your body the fear is located. This is a good practice for body awareness. After you have tapped, you will check in again with your body to notice any changes.

What To Do If The Tapping Isn't Working

As I said, for about half the people the simple technique above does the job. For the rest of you, the reason that your Emotional Meter is not going lower is that there are more "aspects" to your phobia. I call these "bubbles."

Chapter 9: Bubbles

"Fear makes the wolf bigger than he is."
---- German Proverb

Bubbles, bubbles and more bubbles. I don't know what others call them in the field, but I call them bubbles. What are bubbles? Bubbles are the sub issues or other aspects to your phobia connected to the main issues that people have. Read the following case and you will see how sometimes there are multiple aspects attached to our phobias.

Case History

Wes

Issue: "Fear Of Public Restrooms."

A client named Wes, 52 years old, came to me and said that he was tired of having a fear of going into public restrooms. The only time he would ever go into a public restroom was when he was too far from home to "hold it." When he would go into a public restroom his heart would start to pound, and his palms became sweaty. Once in he would rush to do his thing and would rush out without even washing his hands. There was no way he was going to touch anything in there for fear of disease.

In his session, his fear meter put him at an 8 to start with. We begin to tap on the main issue, *"Even though, I have this fear of public restrooms, I love and accept myself."* Etc.

After a few rounds of tapping, he was only at a 7. A few more rounds and he was still at a 7. Since he was stuck at a 7, I knew there must be some other aspect to his phobia that needed to be addressed. I asked him to recall in detail the incident that he feels caused the phobia.

The client thinks a minute and says, "I think it may be because when I was very young, I was at the drive-in movies with my grandpa and he took me to the bathroom during intermission. I touched the soiled toilet seat with my hand. My grandfather yanked my hand away and slapped my face right in front of about 20 other people. My pants were down, and when he yanked me I tripped on my pants and fell. I remember feeling so embarrassed. I was about 6 years old I think.

Then I had to hear a lecture about how diseases are all over public bathrooms. Later when he apologized to me he also had the talk about not going in public restrooms alone because there are bad men who will do bad things to me. Wes said all he wanted to do was go to the bathroom and look at all that happened, how that one little incident messed his mind up for years.

When you are only 6 years old, and a person of authority tells you something, it cements in your mind as truth. Even when you reach the "age of reason" it is hard to get what was "cemented in" out of your head.

We discussed possible "bubbles," and this is what we came up with. The bubbles we tapped on individually were:

- *"Even though, my grandfather embarrassed and humiliated me in front of the other kids in the restroom when I was 6 years old, I love and accept myself."*

- *"Even though, I'm afraid of getting diseases if I go into public restrooms, I love and accept myself."*

- *"Even though, I'm afraid of being molested in a public restroom, I love and accept myself."*

We did all of those 2 times each and then tested to see where his emotions were. We were happy that now he was only at a 2. We stopped the session there. I checked up on him a few months later, and he said he now laughs about having that fear. He is using tapping to help his grandkids with some of their school issues.

So think about what your bubbles might be surrounding your phobia. In your private session you will make a list and then tap on each bubble as a separate issue.

Repetition is good, so let's recap where you are so far.

- You learned what EFT is and heard what all the scientific proof is showing how wonderful it works.

- You watched EFT in action in Rwanda, Haiti, and in relief for PTSD war veterans.

- You learned the tapping points.

- You learned about your inner Emotional Meter

- You learned to check in to see where you feel the emotion and fear in your body.

- You learned that sometimes there are multiple aspects to your phobia and that each aspect needs to be tapped on separately.

Not bad so far. You are getting close to doing your own personal session and getting rid of your phobia. First read the Frequently Asked Questions section below. It will clear up a few things you might still have questions about. After that, I will walk you through your personal session.

Chapter 10: Frequently Asked Questions and Answers

"Courage is not the lack of fear but the ability to face it."

---- Lt. John B. Putnam Jr. (1921-1944)

How many times do I tap each point?

Answer: You can tap about 6 to 9 times on each point. It doesn't matter exactly how many times you tap so don't get hung up on this. You are tapping just enough to get the energy to that area going. You don't need to count as it distracts from the process. Just tap as you are talking and move on to the next point.

How hard do I tap?

Answer: Don't tap too soft or too hard, tap firmly, but not enough to hurt yourself.

What order do I tap in?

Answer: It actually doesn't matter at all in what order you tap. I teach to first tap on the karate point on the side of either hand to establish the issue you are tapping on and then tap from the top of the head down. It's easier for people to remember all the points that way. Once you get proficient at Tapping you can tap in any order you like.

Can I say the wrong thing and make it worse?

Answer: No you can't make it worse. Just be aware as you verbalize some of your issues, the hidden emotional energy that you have is going to start surfacing. You may start to feel very emotional. That is a good thing. As you tap, you will be eliminating this energy and it will never return to that same level again.

After you finish tapping, you will feel like a person does after they have had a "good cry," calm and at peace.

Why do I have to say *"I completely and deeply love and accept myself?*

Answer: Saying *"I love myself,"* is a most powerful statement. We don't know exactly why saying loving and accepting things about yourself works, but it does.

For a lot of people, it is very difficult to say that they love themselves. That in itself is a tapping issue that shows you need to find out why you feel you don't love yourself. Write down the "bubbles"of why you feel you don't love yourself and tap on each one separately. Here is a good way to get comfortable saying that you love yourself. Tap while saying this statement, *" Even though, I have a problem saying I love and accept myself, I am open to the idea that I may in a day or two or a week or so, be able to say it."* Here is another phrase that works with my clients. *"Even though I can't*

say I love and accept myself at this time, I am open to the
idea that I will be able to say it soon."

Can I say other affirmations too?

Answer: Yes you may, all affirmations are welcome. As you are talking out your problems and tapping, stop, go to your higher self, and from that perspective say something positive and loving about yourself. Here is an example: *"Even though, I really hate my husband at the moment and feel like kicking him, I really love and accept myself. I love myself because I am a good person and a good wife; I give my all to this relationship. I'm a really good person, but you know I feel real hatred at the moment. How dare he say what he said to me. Even though, I am so angry right now; I love myself. "*

Don't be overly concerned about having to say particular words, just let the words flow.

Should I say what I am feeling in my statement?

Answer: Yes, yes,yes, saying how or what you feel is crucial. Is it sadness, embarrassment, depressed, helpless, worthless, unimportant, anger, rage, hurt, that you feel? There is a huge range of emotions that we feel. Go to the internet and see the lists of human emotions. Read them and ask yourself which emotions you are feeling and then add them into your statement. *" Even though, I feel a deep sadness about _____ "* etc.

What if I just can't seem to figure out what to say?

Answer: If that is the case just start tapping while you are talking about your issues and how you feel about them. Here is an example. Let's say you are mad at your boss at work because you got passed over for a promotion. Just start talking. *" Even though, I feel so angry for getting passed over for promotion, I love and accept myself. I hate my boss, and maybe he knows that. He is such an idiot. Doesn't he see all the good things I do around the office? I am one of the best workers he* *has. I love myself for being such a good worker. Maybe I will just go in and quit. That will show the son of a bitch. I hate feeling this way. I feel rejected and sad. I was so looking forward to advancing my career. I love myself because I am a good worker. That is the most important thing. I at least have my integrity and know that I am a good worker. I love and accept myself even if my boss doesn't see me that way."*

All the while you are saying these things you are tapping on the different points in any order you wish. You are alternating saying what your true feelings are and then going to your "higher self" and saying loving and accepting things about yourself.

How Honest Do I Need to be About My Feelings?

Answer: I say be brutally honest. Here is an example. I had a client whose father raped her over a period of 6 years. She comes from one of America's richest families, and her father is still alive. He also molested her other sisters. One of her issues was a "fear of men." Here was her starting tapping statement. *"Even though I am angry at my father for molesting me when I was a child that now makes me fear all men, I love and accept myself."* We got nowhere when she said that. After a few rounds with no emotional relief. I said to her that she had to be really, really honest about how she feels about her dad, and put that in her tapping statement. She began to cry, then screamed at the top of her voice, *"EVEN THOUGH, MY FATHER RAPED ME OVER AND OVER WHEN I WAS A HELPLESS CHILD, I HATE THAT BASTARD, AND IF HE WERE HERE NOW, I WOULD BEAT THAT MOTHER FUCKER TO DEATH. I HATE HIM, I HATE HIM. EVEN THOUGH I HATE HIM AND WANT HIM DEAD………. I LOVE AND ACCEPT MYSELF. I LOVE MYSELF EVEN THOUGH I HAVE SUCH HATED IN MY HEART."* All this came out of this sweet, reserved beautiful person.

That was the breakthrough we were looking for. Once she really said what she was feeling, the healing began. She had many issues as you can imagine and lots and lots of bubbles. I am happy to say that she is doing remarkably well. That is why I love this job so much.

Don't hold back and don't be embarrassed to be human. If you hate someone rather than dislike them, say you hate them. If you need to cuss, let it out. You will see how great it feels to be honest with how you really feel and then forgive yourself for feeling that way. Honesty pays great rewards in the healing process.

How many rounds of tapping do I have to do?

Answer: Every issue is different. I have clients who have gone from a 10 to a zero in only one round on some of their issues, but usually it will take multiple rounds. I would say do two or three complete rounds. Then take a breath, take a sip of water and then close your eyes.

Look at your inner scale now and see where the needle goes. Most of the time it will be less than before you started the tapping. Let's say it was a 10, and now you feel it is a 6 or 7. You will go Hmm to yourself; this is working. Now do a few more rounds and see where it is. In most cases, it will continually go down. If you are stuck and the needle isn't moving, then it is because you have another "bubble" to take care of.

Once you discover the new bubble, you tap on that until it goes down. Then go back to your original statement and tape again. Almost always, your needle on the main issue will have gone down some more. Sometimes a major issue will have a lot of bubbles attached to it. It is like peeling an onion. You must keep peeling the layers away to get your excess negative emotion down as close to zero as you can.

What if I tap and my fear level doesn't go down?

Answer: If it is not going down it is because of the "bubbles" attached to your main issue. Read the previous answer above again or back to the chapter on "Bubbles."

What if the level goes down only a little and is stuck no matter how much I tap?

Answer: Again, as in the above two questions, if you don't seem to be going anywhere there is something about the issue that you haven't discovered. It could be a bubble you haven't discovered or as I talked about in an earlier chapter, it is possible it may be a carry over from a previous lifetime. I have had only a few clients in years that got stuck and no matter what we did nothing happened. As I mentioned EFT is miraculous, but it is not a panacea.

What if I have done everything you say and still have my phobia?

Answer: If that is the case I want to invite you to email me. I will send you my phone information, and we can do a session over the phone or with Skype. Phone sessions work as well as" in person" sessions most of the time. My fees are very reasonable and success guaranteed. If you don't feel you've made an improvement, there is no charge.

Can I use tapping on some of my other issues?

Answer: Yes you can use it for other issues. I use it every day for minor and major stress issues. Remember what I said about the recent studies that showed your Cortisol (stress hormone) levels drop significantly when you tap. Here are some other issues that EFT can help you with.

- Addictive Cravings, including food, cigarettes, alcohol, and drugs

- Pain Relief & Physical Healing

- Post Traumatic Stress

- Disorder Children's Issues

- Grief, Guilt, Loss and Love Pain

- Allergies, Breathing Difficulties

- Learning Disorders; including Dyslexia, ADHD, etc.

- Fears and Phobias; including fear of flying, heights, dogs, etc.

- Insomnia, Anxiety, Anger

- Procrastination & Indecisiveness

- Concentration & relaxation

- Confidence & self-esteem

EFT is also good for taking away excess daily stress that comes up in your life. I use it before going into auditions for movie roles. In the last two years I have not blown one audition. I get more roles in movies because I have taken the fear out of auditioning.

Chapter 11: One More Interesting Case

"What are fears but voices airy?
Whispering harm where harm is not.
And deluding the unwary
Till the fatal bolt is shot!"
---- Wordsworth

Here is one more interesting case that shows you what to expect with EFT.

Case History

Issue: Fear of Taking Tests

Abby

I met a woman named Abby at a party back in 2009 and in our conversation I found out she was to take the Bar Exam in two days to become a lawyer. She said she had failed it twice already and was terrified of taking it again for a fear of failing once more. She was already working in a law office, and the lawyer was actually letting her work as a lawyer in some aspects, even though by law she wasn't supposed to be doing those things. They let her do that because she was brilliant and they knew she was taking the Bar soon. After all, she was already very good at her lawyer skills. She seemed a "natural".

What her bosses didn't know was that she suffered from "test anxiety." Having test anxiety has nothing to do with being smart. It's a whole other thing. In Abby's case, it was a "fear of failure," that equated to having "test anxiety."

We figured out that her phobias came from her teenage years. She flunked her drivers test six times when she was a teenager. When she would be driving with her mom or dad in the car and preparing for the test she was as cool as a cucumber. The problem came when the Tester started writing notes on his notepad while she was driving. Her fear of failing took over and she made all kinds of mistakes. It became a self fulling prophecy.

On her 7th try to get her license, the Tester felt so sorry for her that he just let her pass. That's one of the benefits of living in a small town where everyone knows everyone.

With the Bar Exam in only two days, she was starting to panic. She was on her third drink at the party, and she told me she's not even a drinker. I told her what I did, that I specialized in ridding people of their fears and phobias, and she said, "Please will you help me?" Abby said if she didn't pass the test she was going to lose her job. I made an appointment the next day which was the eve of her taking the test. It was "do or die" for her.

She was a tough one. Remember how I mentioned "bubbles," the issues around your fears and phobias. It took us a few hours to uncover what they were. Here are the different bubbles we had to tap on.

- *"Even though, I have this fear of taking the bar exam because I might fail, I love and accept myself."*

- *"Even though, I'm afraid to take the test because I will look and feel stupid in front of my boss, I love and accept myself."*

- *"Even though, I'm afraid to take the test because I might lose my job, I love and accept myself."*

- *"Even though, I'm afraid to take the test because I will look like a failure in front of my children if don't pass, I love and accept myself."*

We got her fear meter down from a 10 at first to a 5 and that is ok, but not enough to make sure she would pass the test. We started talking some more about how important this job was and what it meant for her kids. She was a single mom. She had gotten out of an abusive relationship 5 years earlier and struggled so much to get by. Her ex was trying to take her kids, and the only reason that the judge was letting her keep the kids was that she was in law school. Abby was a loving mother, but if she couldn't work, she couldn't provide for her children. On the other hand, her ex was very well off. He was a very controlling man and had always had to have things his way.

Then the light went on in my head. I said to her say this, *"Even though, I am afraid of failing the test and losing my children, I completely and deeply love and accept myself."* She fell apart emotionally as she tried to say those words. I held her as she wept. We stopped for about five minutes as she regained her composure and then started again. This time she was able to get through it. She said, *"I'm so afraid of losing my kids, and even though I may lose them, I love and accept myself."* We did three rounds of that and ended up with a positive round of tapping. As she tapped, the different points I had her say.

- *"Even though, I have all these different fears, I love and accept myself."*

- *"I know that I am smart and know all the material."*

- *"It feels good to know that I am intelligent after all look how my bosses have so much confidence in me. They are even letting me act as a lawyer even when I am not one."*

- *"It feels so nice to have a boss that really believes in me."*

- *"I am a wonderful, loving mother and I will always do what it takes to take care of my kids."*

After these rounds of tapping I tested her and she was at a 2. We both felt so relieved.

Are you starting to see how this works? I will say again. You have to explore yourself and find out what all the "bubbles" are that are attached to your fear. You treat each bubble as a separate issue and tap on them separately. You keep on checking in and testing to see where your emotional needle is until you get it down to an acceptable level.

Abby left that day and I didn't hear from her for a few weeks.

I forgot to tell you something about myself. Before I became a Hypnotherapist, I was a Corporate Comedian and Fake Motivational Speaker for over 30 years. I still get a good gig once in a while even though I am not pursuing being a comedian anymore.

A few weeks after seeing Abby I was at the Wynn Casino doing a Custom Comedy Show for a major US Bank.

After the show I was in my suite, and I get this call from a screaming woman. It startled me for a second and then I heard her scream, " I passed the test! I passed the test!!!!" She was so overjoyed. I felt so happy for her too.

She said when she was taking the test and her fear started to rise, she would stop the test, close her eyes and tap while saying, *"Even though, I still have a little bit of fear about taking this test I deeply and completely love and accept myself."* Then she would do a round of, *"I am such a loving mother, and I am going to pass this test to keep my children. I love and accept myself because I am a caring and loving mother."*

She got 92% on the test. How cool is that! She used what she learned in our session. When her excess emotions were getting the best of her she tapped them away. You will find yourself using EFT almost daily to help you get through emotional situations.

See what happens when you deal with your fears. The love for her children was what motivated her to do whatever was necessary to pass the test.

Chapter 12: It's Time for Your Private Session

"I must not fear. Fear is the mind-killer. Fear is the little-death that brings total obliteration. I will face my fear. I will permit it to pass over me and through me. And when it has gone past I will turn the inner eye to see its path. Where the fear has gone, there will be nothing. Only I will remain."

--- Frank Herbert, Dune - Bene Gesserit Litany Against Fear

Pick a private area in your home, a place where you feel the most comfortable to have your session. If you have others in the house, let them know not to interrupt you for an hour. If you have small children, it may be best to drop them off at the sitters for a few hours. Some of my clients like to have some soft background music playing in their session, others find it too distracting, so do what makes you feel the most comfortable.

I suggest having a note pad next to you in case you have an inspiration and need to make any notes. Turn off all the ringers to your phones. Also, go to the bathroom and drink some water before you start.

If you are a spiritual person, I suggest that you take a few minutes and say a prayer. Also, have a minute of gratitude for all the blessings in your life. If you meditate, do a 20 or 30 minute meditation. I have noted in my personal therapy practice that people, who have a strong spiritual belief, recover from their issues much faster than those who don't. Let's get started.

Chapter 13: Your Personal Session

Before you do your actual session, read the routine below several times first, so you know exactly what you are going to be doing. Then come back to this page and begin your session.

Now, sit in a comfortable chair or sit up in bed with a pillow behind you. Have some tissues nearby in case you need them. Make sure your water is next to you. Take three deep breaths and close your eyes.

1. Focus on your phobia. Take a minute and really think about it. Imagine yourself in a scenario where you have to deal with your phobia or relive the event that caused your phobia. Really get into it. Then rate the intensity on a 0-10 scale. Also make note of where in your body the intense feeling is located.

2. While tapping on the Karate Chop point say this three times. *"Even though, I have this (state the problem) _____, I completely and deeply love and accept myself."* Continually tap on this first point until you have repeated the phrase three times.

3. Tap on each of the tapping points 5 -8 times, starting from the point on top of the head, while repeating the problem. At two or three of the points in every round, be sure to add *"I completely and deeply love and accept myself."* When you say that, say it with enthusiasm. Your subconscious needs to really hear you. The more feeling you put into it the better your results will be.

4. Do two or three complete rounds of the tapping. Then take a sip of water, sit back and close your eyes. Now re-rate your emotional intensity. If it is

not down to an acceptable level, do a few more rounds and re-rate again.

5. Again, if you can't think of any causes, EFT will still work. It might take a little longer, but you should start to notice a difference in the emotional charge to your phobia. One phrase to use that will help if your emotional meter is stuck at a certain number is this: *"Even though, I don't have a clue why I have this phobia, I still love and accept myself."* Or try this one: *" I am OK with not knowing why I have this phobia and I am willing to let go of it. I no longer wish to have it in my life, I love myself for letting go of it."*

6. If your emotional level is still at an uncomfortable level, begin tapping on the "bubbles" that you have identified as a probable cause for your fear. Think of each issue and take an emotional meter reading, just as you did for the first issue you tapped on. Start at the beginning and repeat this whole

procedure with each bubble as an individual issue until you get it to an acceptable level.

Note: A few people have told me that they only had moderate success in the tapping, but the relief that they achieved, lowered their stress levels enough that they were able to get through their phobic episodes easier and with less stress and drama.

One of my clients was at a 9 on "fear of flying." He didn't know why he was afraid, but he refused to fly anywhere. We worked for about two hours trying everything we could think of, and we were only able to get him down to a 5. He said a 5 was a lot better than a 9.

He had gotten his fear reduced enough that he got on a plane and went to see his granddaughter graduate a few weeks later. On the flight, he had some anxiety, but not enough to put him in panic mode. So you see, you don't have to get your level all the way down to zero to get the benefits of EFT. Even hardcore cases get some benefits from tapping.

I know that if we were able to do another session we could get his "5" down even lower, but he says he is fine now since he probably won't ever have to fly again anyway.

Chapter 14: Wrapping Things Up

My personal success rate at getting phobias to go away or to at least get them to an acceptable level is about 90%. My colleagues and other therapist are reporting about the same percentages in their practices.

I am hoping the process you have just learned will empower you to make other positive changes in your life. Now you can use EFT to help you cope with your day to day struggles

Please share your successes, questions, or concerns with me. This is the first edition of this book, and as with everything in life, improvements can always be made. Let me know if you have an idea of how I might improve this process. If you think I need to be clearer or state things in a more understandable or different way, let me know. You will see my email on the last page.

Hypnotherapy & Energy Psychology

Phone and Skype Sessions Available

Email me at   ReganForston@yahoo.com

Yes, Hypnosis does work over the phone. I have been using phone sessions and Skype for years to help people completely change their lives. We are in a new age of awareness. Dr. Oz recently stated that Energy Medicine is the future of medicine.

I am a trained EFT (Tapping) practitioner. Emotional Freedom Technique or EFT is now the fastest healing modality used in the world. It is now accepted by the National Psychological Association. I teach you how to do it for yourself. Fears and Phobias can be gone almost instantly. My PTSD (Post Traumatic Stress Disorder) clients heal very quickly. It only takes weeks or months instead of years as in traditional therapies to make significant progress. I can help you with any of the issues below.

Post Traumatic Stress

Fears and Phobias

Stop Smoking

Lose Weight

Relationship Issues

Grief Counseling

Anger Management

Stress Relief   (One of my specialties)

Pain Management

Past Life Regression

Self Esteem Issues

Email me and I will give you my contact number. I can start helping you immediately. I have clients all over the world.

Sincerely,

Regan Forston Ct. Ht. (Certified Hypnotherapist)

ReganForston@yahoo.com

www.ingramcontent.com/pod-product-compliance
Lightning Source LLC
Chambersburg PA
CBHW070650290526
45790CB00001B/254